Milestones

Also by Marina Tsvetaeva
in Christopher Whyte's translation

Moscow in the Plague Year (Archipelago, New York)

Marina Tsvetaeva

Milestones

translated from the Russian
by
Christopher Whyte

Shearsman Books

First published in the United Kingdom in 2015 by
Shearsman Books
50 Westons Hill Drive
Emersons Green
BRISTOL
BS16 7DF

Shearsman Books Ltd Registered Office
30–31 St. James Place, Mangotsfield, Bristol BS16 9JB
(this address not for correspondence)

www.shearsman.com

ISBN 978-1-84861-416-1

Contents

Introduction   9

Milestones *(first published 1922)*

'I opened the small iron box'   27
'I planted a young apple tree'   28
'I went out to the lake. Its banks were steep'   29
'No-one went off with anything!'   30
'Seeing off the ones I love'   31
'You throw your head back when you laugh'   32
'What can it be disarms me so?'   33
'The mirror shattered into silver'   34
'Snow takes more than a day to melt'   35
'Silver doves, scattering, soar in the evening sky'   36
'Never stop making up'   37
'Before autumn, no giddy wind'   38
'Ruined by a woman. Look'   39
'The strangest malady took hold of him'   40
'My canopies are covered with'   41
'I go out to the porch and listen'   42
'On Annunciation day'   43
'Tomorrow's the Annunciation'   44
'In your fourth year'   47
'Checking the girls, so in the jug the kvass'   49
'Dimitry! Marina! In all the world'   50

Poems about Moscow
1. 'Clouds all around'   53
2. 'Take from my hands a city no hands built'   54
3. 'Squares rush us at top speed'   55
4. 'One day – people maintain, a sad one – they'll'   56
5. 'Across the city which Peter rejected'   57
6. 'Over the blue haze of the woods round Moscow'   58
7. 'Seven hills resembling seven bells!'   59
8. 'Moscow! Enormous city'   60
9. 'The rowan tree flared'   61

'Bent over double from sheer badness' 62
'Seeing his scattered locks' 63
'Drink and eat, be of good cheer!' 64
'Roads go in all directions' 65
'My soul's a tempting bait, they give me tender' 67
'As long as you're with me, you won't get bored!' 68
'Sleeplessness has traced a shadow ring' 69
'You could have been my mother in those days' 71
'I came to you at dead of night' 72
'Roll up! Roll up! Roll up!' 73

POEMS TO BLOK
1. 'Your name's a bird caught in the hand' 74
2. 'Kindly phantom' 75
3. 'You take your way past with the setting sun' 77
4. 'A beast needs its lair' 78
5. 'Here in my Moscow – domes burning bright!' 79
6. 'Concluding that he must be human' 80
7. 'The village where I used to live' 81
8. 'Gadflies swarm around indifferent jades' 82

'I adore kissing' 83

POEMS TO AKHMATOVA
1. 'Muse of weeping, loveliest of the muses!' 84
2. 'Head held between my hands, I stand–' 85
3. 'One further immense sweep, and then' 86
4. 'The boy's called Leo' 87
5. 'So many followers and friends!' 88
6. 'I won't be left behind! You are the guard' 89
7. 'You, who tear the covers off' 90
8. 'People were shouting at the fair' 91
9. 'Anna Chrysostom of the Golden Lips' 92
10. 'A voice today in the thin wire above' 93
11. 'You catch hold of my sun high in' 94

'They gave me hands to stretch towards everyone' 95

'The sun's bleached pale. The clouds are low. Behind'   96
'In this immense city of mine – night'   97
'After a night without sleep the whole body is weaker'   98
'Now I'm a heavenly guest'   99
'Yet again'   100
'A female adventurer, a man'   101

DANIEL
1. 'I sat on the sill, dangling my legs'   102
2. 'Women on horseback, ruins, psalms'   103
3. 'In the full moon the horses snorted'   104

'Tonight I'm alone in the night, a nun'   105
'Oh, how delicate and faint'   106
'Not something I can get worked up about'   107
'Dark as a pupil, and absorbing light'   108
'Stooping from his troubles, God'   109
'A thin wing from the hooded cape'   110
'Shedding no pointless tears'   111
'I kiss leaves burnished crimson and sleepy mouths'   112
'Hold on a moment, friend!'   113
'If fate had wanted us to be united'   114
'Every day's a Saturday for me!'   115
'Along paths gently resonant with frost'   116
'Who sleeps when night falls? Nobody can sleep!'   117
'Look – another window'   118

Notes   120

Introduction

This collection is a lyrical diary from the final year of Tsarist Russia, before the twin revolutions of February and October 1917 transformed the country beyond all hope of recognition, and irrevocably. A young woman of 23 grapples with motherhood and marriage, with love, sex and friendship, with the traditions of the Orthodox church and her own instinctive polytheism, with the literary environment where she is reaching maturity and, last but not least, with the dimensions of her talent.

*

Marina Tsvetaeva offered Yury Ivask this account of her background in a letter dated May 12th 1934:

> Generally speaking, make no mistake, there's not much in me that's Russian (NB! something everyone gets wrong in the heat of the moment), even my blood is—excessively—mixed: my maternal grandfather (Alexander Davidovich Meyn)—was a Baltic German, with some Serbian blood, my grandmother (born Bernatskaya) was pure Polish, I have nothing Russian on my mother's side, and on my father's side—*everything*. That's how *I* came out: either not one bit, or everything. Even in spiritual terms, I'm a halfblood.

When Maria Meyn, who was a gifted pianist, married Ivan Tsvetaev, he was a man of 45, a widower with a son and daughter, still very much in love with his first wife. The son of an obscure country priest, he rose to become Professor of Art Theory and History at Moscow University, and was the moving spirit behind the foundation of the Alexander III Museum of Fine Arts (renamed the Pushkin Museum after the revolution). 21 years his junior, Tsvetaeva's mother had given her heart to a married man her father forbade her to frequent. It was a marriage of duty. She became her husband's eager helpmate in work on the museum, travelling to the Ural Mountains with him to choose marble for the pillars of its façade. Marina claimed to have been treated with a harshness which their mother spared her younger sister Anastasiya (Asya). Their mother, who suffered from tuberculosis, took both daughters to Nervi by Genoa in Liguria, to Lausanne and to the Black Forest, where it was hoped the milder climate could arrest the progress of her disease. Unexpected relief from the prospect of spending Easter Sunday confined to their hated pension in Freiburg was provided by a surprise visit to Rainer Maria Rilke's friend and patron, Marie von Thurn und Taxis, dedicatee of the *Duino Elegies*.

Before her death in 1906, Tsvetaeva's mother arranged for her daughters not to receive their inheritance till they were 40, in case their radical sympathies should lead them to hand the funds over to a revolutionary cause. They were unable to touch the money before it disappeared in 1917. That there were darker notes to family life in the house at Three Ponds Lane in Moscow is clear from two deliberately mysterious references in Tsvetaeva's correspondence with Boris Pasternak. The first comes in a letter dated November 1st 1927:

> By the way, some time I'll tell you about my childhood, something happened which no-one knows about, not my mother on her deathbed, something Asya will never get to know.

And the second in a letter dated March 4th 1928:

> Change of subject. If you are to grasp me at a different level, the right one for me, I would have to tell you things which it is not possible to write down, I am too much of a coward, my hand doesn't dare. My hand lacking courage – hand? my tongue – has ruined my life. Due to the impossibility of saying.
>
>   But inside I howled and shouted (it howled and shouted) from the first minute. Boris, try to understand:

all my life, at a given moment, I find myself neither free nor tethered, a woman and not a woman, not *some*one's and not anyone's, having lost the place in spite of all my precision… Of course there are ugly words, and here the formal method would offer great help. The most important thing: I see it all with wondrous clarity: a doctor of genius bending over a patient for whom there is no hope (what, in fact, I said about Proust).

What proved impossible to say, what the 'ugly words' would have defined, we shall probably never know. The extreme hypothesis, some form of sexual abuse, might explain Tsvetaeva's erratic emotional and sexual behaviour in adult life, along with the difficulty she experienced in achieving any adequate form of relationship stability. There are rumours of two suicide attempts in adolescence, one of them planned to take place in the theatre during a performance by the actress Sarah Bernhardt, and foiled by the pistol failing to go off. Aged 15, she wrote to her friend Yury Yurkievich that only the prospect of revolution could reconcile her to staying alive.

Tsvetaeva's first book of poems, *Evening Album*, was published at her own expense in 1910. It brought her the attention of poet and painter Maksimilian Voloshin, who accepted paying guests in the house at Koktebel in Crimea where he lived with his mother. This became the centre of a colony of artists and writers, and it was on the beach there that Tsvetaeva glimpsed, in the summer of 1911, an astonishingly handsome, tall yet frail young man. She challenged him to choose a pebble for her from those on the strand, and claimed his choice confirmed her decision to marry him. Sergey Yakovlevich Efron was of part-Jewish origin. Both his parents had a history of revolutionary activism. His mother at one point belonged to an extremist terrorist organisation called the Maximalists. Living in exile in Paris, she came home one day in January 1910 to find her son Constantine had hanged himself, and immediately did the same. One of Tsvetaeva's last concerns, before leaving Paris to return to the Soviet Union in June 1939, was to put in order the grave in the Montparnasse cemetery of the woman who, if she had known her, would have been her mother-in-law. The photograph she took of the slab, with the projected, outline shadow of Tsvetaeva's hat and head, survives.

Her father's initial opposition having been overcome ('A conversation repeated down the centuries!', she commented to Voloshin) she and Efron were married in January 1912, and set off on a honeymoon which took them via various locations on the Italian peninsula as far as Sicily. Their first daugher Ariadne (Alya) was born in September 1912. Tsvetaeva's father died the following August.

It is hard to conceive of the degree of liberty Tsvetaeva enjoyed in the years following her mother's death. She and her sister were in the habit of reciting her poems in unison, in singsong voices, until asked to stop because audiences found it so distracting. Their mother had insisted the girls should grow up speaking French and German as well as Russian. While still a teenager, Tsvetaeva read Nietzsche's *Thus Spake Zarathustra* – she is said to have recited Pushkin to a nanny when aged 6 – but reserved her fervour for more questionable figures, such as Marie Bashkirtseva and Edmond Rostand. Aged 16, she journeyed on her own to spend a summer in Paris. Heartbroken when her French instructress failed to reciprocate a passionate attachment, she rented a room in the Rue Napoleon solely because of the name. Years afterwards, in a letter to Aleksandr Bakhrakh dated January 10th 1924, she would recall how

> Often, wrapped in thought, I went into the opposite doorway, and the concierge, with a smile, would say: *Mademoiselle se trompe souvent de porte.* (Thus perhaps, by chance, will I end up in Heaven instead of Hell!)

Tsvetaeva clearly saw her commitment to the chronically ineffectual, artistically inclined, tuberculotic Efron as a lifelong one. This did not, however, exclude a protracted series of extramarital involvements, impassioned even when denied physical realisation, which marked her existence, and fuelled her poetry, at least as far as 1924. The first may well have concerned her husband's elder brother Pyotr, who was in exile from 1907 to 1913 and died from tuberculosis in Moscow in summer 1914. Among the most clamorous was a relationship with the poet Sophia Parnok (accented on the second syllable), seven years her senior, which began in the autumn of 1915 and lasted for nearly a year and a half.

*

The start of 1916 found the two women in St Petersburg, renamed Petrograd since the onset of hostilities with Germany. Tsvetaeva could not get over the fact that people in the northern capital never seemed to sleep, or the sheer quantity of poetry that was recited, also by herself. She met practically everyone of note in the literary world, with the sole exception of Anna Akhmatova. Having left an ailing Parnok to go out and hear Mikhail Kuzmin recite his poems, she returned to find the woman who took her place in Parnok's life sitting on the bed. Kuzmin had read in the home of the Kannegisers, whose son Leonid would later assassinate the Soviet Chief of Police Uritsky, in revenge for the killing by the Cheka of his own male lover. *Milestones* contains just one poem addressed to Parnok, 'You could have been my mother in those days', immediately followed by an abject, coded request to return to Efron's side, 'I came to you at dead of night'.

In St Petersburg Tsvetaeva also made the acquaintance of the young Osip Mandelstam. He went to Moscow so frequently during the spring that a friend jokingly enquired whether he had taken a job with the railway company. If there can be no doubting the profound impression his work made upon her, Tsvetaeva's attitude to Mandelstam was indulgent, even condescending, corroborated by a comic account of a disastrous visit in a letter to one of Sergey's sisters dated June 12th 1916:

The day was taken up with him complaining about fate, while we comforted and praised him, with eating and with news of the literary world. In the evening—

actually, it was night—he somehow quietened down, lay on the deer's hide and started being unpleasant. Finally tiring of him, Asya and I left him to his own devices and sat down in the far corner of the room—Mavry Aleksandrovich, Asya and me. Asya started telling the story of *Corinne* in her own words, while we guffawed like mad. Then we proposed Mandelstam should eat something. He jumped up, as if someone had bitten him: 'What's this then! I can't eat all day long! I'm going out of my mind! Why did I come here? I've had enough! I want to leave right now! I've really had enough!'

They were in Aleksandrovskoye, where Tsvetaeva first read Akhmatova in depth, and wrote a miraculous sequence of poems which Akhmatova was said to have carried around in her handbag for years, in Tsvetaeva's tattered handwritten copy. There she also wrote 'The sun's bleached pale. The clouds are low. Behind', one of very few poems where she refers to the disastrous war being fought against German and Austro-Hungarian forces far to the west, to which fresh troops were being transported by train.

Under the effect of Tsvetaeva's infatuation with the poet Tikhon Churilin, Efron, then a student at Moscow University, applied to join up as a volunteer in March. His year was called up the following month and, having been declared medically fit, he was assigned to the ensigns' academy. Bureaucratic delays meant he was required to present himself every five days without receiving clear directions as to where to go. His health worsened. Dreaming of a quiet life on an estate outside Moscow, he left with his sister for a sanatorium in the Caucasus in August. Only in January of the following year would he finally set off for Nizhny Novgorod. Meanwhile Tsvetaeva was translating a novel by Anna de Noailles which began serial publication in *Northern Notebooks* in September.

In Moscow, on May 3rd 1941, not quite four months before she committed suicide, Tsvetaeva made annotations in a copy of *Milestones* giving the names of the individuals behind specific items. 'Silver doves, scattering, soar in the evening sky…', 'Never stop making up' and 'Not autumn yet. No giddy wind' were addressed to Churilin, who had already spent several years in a mental asylum, and is described by Simon Karlinsky as 'an authentic surrealist before such a category was invented'. Tsvetaeva considered him the best poet of the war, and told Pasternak, in a letter dated February 14th 1923, that when they met

> I got the feeling: I can swear to his future – he ruined it! Beyond hope! He tortured his genius, tearing the feathers from its wings.

Mandelstam is the addressee of the poems from 'No-one went off with anything!' as far as 'What can it be disarms me so?', as well as of the first three 'Poems to Moscow'. It would seem reasonable to add the fifth – concerning which Tsvetaeva observed in February 1939 that there had in fact been no rejection, she merely decided it would sound better like this – as well as 'Ruined by a woman. Look' and 'The strangest malady took hold of him'. Beneath 'They gave me hands to stretch towards everyone', which follows immediately after the 'Poems to Akhmatova', Tsvetaeva wrote:

> All the poems from here until the end of the book – and many later on – were written for Nikodim Plutser-Sarna, of whom I may say, now a life has gone by, that he dared to love me, dared to love that troubling phenomenon – me.

Plutser-Sarna was an economist who spoke Russian with a pronounced Polish accent. Tsvetaeva's letters to him have been partially reconstructed from her notebooks. In autumn 1918 she told him that

> A woman, if she is a human being, needs a man as a luxury – very, very occasionally. Books, her home, caring for her children, the joy they give her, solitary

walks, painful moments, moments of ecstasy – what has all of this to do with men?

Besides men, a woman has two unbounded seas: what matters in her life, and her own soul.

Transcribing the annotation into her notebook for the year 1941, Tsvetaeva added 'plus quite a few *before*' to 'and many later on'. Plutser-Sarna inspired the figure of the Protestant divine in 'Daniel', who meets his end due to witchcraft practised by the baffling, red-haired young woman who is his companion. During the years of appalling hardship and crushing poverty subsequent to the Bolshevik Revolution, in the period known as War Communism, he and his wife Tatyana offered sterling support to Tsvetaeva, whose husband was fighting far from Moscow in the counter-revolutionary forces. Tatyana is probably the addressee of a haunting, uncollected lyric dated September 8th, 1916, which begins

A time will come, rival of mine, when I'll
pay you a visit on a moonlit night,
while frogs can be heard wailing from the pond,
and pity drives women out of their minds.

When contact with Yurkevich was resumed in summer 1916, looking back to their earlier friendship, Tsvetaeva observed (letter dated July 21st):

How miserable I was then! A tragic childhood and a blessed youth.

And she summed her present condition up as follows:

And I want lightness, freedom, understanding—not to hold anyone back and for no-one to hold me back! My whole life long I've been in love with my own soul, with the city where I live, with a tree at the end of the road – with the air. And I feel infinitely happy.

At this stage at least, the balance was overwhelmingly positive.

*

The poems with which *Milestones* opens are not explicitly autobiographical. Tsvetaeva introduces motifs from folklore and fairy-tale, preferring liminal settings such as the porch of a house, or the banks of a lake. Her heroine appears alone, significantly tossing into the stormy waters the ring she has been wearing. Its meanings are not specified, but must include commitment and submission to the law. Birds in general, and swans in particular, evoke escape towards utter freedom, innocence and, through the implicit link with quills and the production of text, poetry itself. Religious settings and motifs are integrated into a vision which has little connection to Christianity or orthodox religious teaching. Tsvetaeva is drawn instinctively to derelicts and social outcasts, as in 'Snow takes more than a day to melt'. Her development of this sympathy is marked by two elements. One could be described as verbal masochism, a vein of self-castigation palpable in most of her mature production. And so, in a prayer on behalf of Tsvetaeva's daughter to a Madonna who is very much the focus of women's solidarity and spirituality:

> Keep her safe from gorgeous language,
> so people won't take her for
> a bird of prey, a witch, like me.

On the other hand, the female outcasts whose voice she assumes, proclaiming their promiscuity to the four winds, revelling in their insubordination where morality and convention are concerned, represent an oneiric dream of a life of unbridled sensuality and freedom, which Tsvetaeva's Calvinist conscience would inevitably step in to prevent her from leading. One of the Mandelstam poems reads like a grimmer version of Coleridge's 'Kubla Khan'. There can be no doubt that poetic inspiration induces a privileged state of trance which sets whoever it affects apart from the world of everyday. Echoes of Zeus and Ganymede, however, intervene in the 'bird with golden eyes' which is 'busy honing its sharp beak', and which seems to be getting ready to turn the chosen one into a prey, a victim. The immediately preceding poem, again with a male protagonist, insists that the very fact he possesses a gift will make a target of the poet. Despite his kinship to the eagles, he is fated to meet a violent end on the scaffold.

'Checking the girls, so in the jug the kvass' is an exquisite evocation of old Russia, in the spirit of the painter Ryabushkin's colourful and forceful representations of peasant life. Three poems couched in a form of free verse culminate in a celebration of two notorious outcasts whose doings formed the material of Pushkin's play *Boris Godunov*, and of the opera Modest Mussorgsky drew from it. Tsvetaeva makes no attempt to whitewash the Polish princess Marina Mnishek, her namesake. Nor does she conceal the admiration which she feels. Mnishek married the pretender to the throne, who insisted he was Dimitry, son of Ivan the Terrible. After a reign of only ten months, he was murdered. Claiming he had miraculously survived, Mnishek produced a second husband and pretender, then died in prison after attempting to proclaim the first man's son as heir. At this point the Romanov dynasty assumed control of Russia. For Tsvetaeva, this woman is the 'lodestar to my tempests', with familiar allegations of black magic and spells.

Looking back across a distance of two decades, Tsvetaeva perceived the significance of her poems about pre-revolutionary Moscow. In a letter dated January 25th 1937 she told Ivask:

> Yes, in 1916 I was the first to speak thus of Moscow. (And, so far, the last, it would seem). It makes me happy and proud, for that was Moscow of the last hour and time. *A farewell.* "...the Georgian Virgin's heart / gleams in a pure gold frame." And will burn—eternally. Those lines were prophetic. *Read them over* and don't forget *the dates.*

She had an especially strong identification with the poem which closes the sequence, somehow emblematic of herself:

That's one of my favourite poems, the most *mine*. Actually, I could have written 'praised', or 'repeated', but no - 'engaged in dispute'! They were contending for my soul, which *everyone* and *no-one* got. (All *gods* and not one *church*!)

At the outset, the 'Poems about Moscow' are coloured by Tsvetaeva's near-romance with Mandelstam. Then fascination with bells pealing from the city steeples, with the nuns, beggars, pilgrims, quack-doctors and convicts who account for so much of its population, takes over. Her invitation to the priest to stuff her mouth with earth shows a characteristic tendency to self-denigration. The fourth poem, however, intones a powerful posthumous address from a noblewoman named Marina, who has at last supplanted the Madonna in one of the city's numerous shrines.

Poems where assumed voices articulate a range of defiant, outcast, stigmatised or even criminal positions are frequent. It would be erroneous to project the boasts of promiscuity ('Not a day but I turn up at the font!') back onto the poet, attractive as the sarcastic scoffing when 'the Virgin with Three Hands' rejects conventional feminine roles undoubtedly is. Tsvetaeva's speakers warn us repeatedly to beware of having dealings with them ('devils will turn up to haul me off', 'I never slept alone', 'At night I didn't keep away/ from places that were cursed'). On the roads to which the title of the collection presumably refers, princes and princesses rub shoulders with cripples and criminals, victims of a shared fate which still leaves room for love and sex. It is tempting to interpret the market stallholder in 'Roll up! Roll up! Roll up!' as the poet Tsvetaeva, hoping to interest readers in the dubious wares she is hawking.

The cycles addressed to Aleksandr Blok and to Anna Akhmatova are public poems, no less than the 'Poems about Moscow'. Thanks to a cunning, utterly serious gambit, by expressing esteem and conferring praise, Tsvetaeva with a single move takes her place alongside those of her contemporaries for whom she had the most regard. The achievement which these poems constitute serves to underline the value of her praise. There is no trace of complaisance, no sentimentalism or self-indulgence. A note of danger underpins both cycles, symptomatic of Tsvetaeva's willingness to take risks in her writing, a failure or even absence of the crucial instinct for self-preservation. So the resonance of Blok's name is likened to 'a trigger clicking at the temple', and the abasement when she falls to her knees before 'the undisputed ruler of my soul' is echoed in the sadistic imagery of the last poem but one. The Akhmatova cycle takes the assumption of intimacy that bit too far. Akhmatova is a 'black sorceress! Oppressor of serfs!' Her consummate skill as poet 'throttles me,/ a tightening belt'. Tsvetaeva compares their relationship to a sentenced prisoner and the guard accompanying him on his journey to Siberia.

Blok was the most outstanding Symbolist poet of Russia's pre-revolutionary Silver Age. From a privileged background, his marriage to the woman he repeatedly idealised in his poetry may never have been consummated. One of his most famous lyrics depicts a prostitute emerging from the smoke of a departing train into a cheap station buffet. Often considered to have predicted the upheavals of 1917 in an almost supernatural fashion, Avril Pyman relates how he commented to Korney Chukovsky, months before his death in 1921, that 'She's gulped me down at last, that filthy, grunting, own-mother of mine Russia, like a sow her piglet'. An epic sequence celebrating a squad of twelve Red guards, like the twelve apostles, ends ambiguously with the image of Christ accompanying them in their riotous frolics. Tsvetaeva portrays Blok as prophet, priest and sacrificial victim, all rolled into one. The third poem in the cycle, as Robin Kimball points out, skilfully recasts a prayer from the Orthodox Vespers by Sophronius, Patriarch of Jerusalem.

Akhmatova was famous for love lyrics placed on the lips of a wistful, melancholic, at times victimised speaker, characterised by a gravity of moral witness which would stand her in great stead when, under Stalin and after the Second World War, she strove to articulate an entire nation's experience of totalitarianism and, in *Poem without a Hero*, offered her own idiosyncratic, riveting and haunting recollection of the pre-revolutionary years in St Petersburg. In both cycles, Tsvetaeva performs the extraordinary feat of reproducing the tonality and mood of another poet, while at the same time coming up with texts that are unmistakably her own.

At the end of the second of two readings which Blok gave in Moscow, on May 9th and 14th 1920, Tsvetaeva instructed her daughter Alya to place an envelope containing a manuscript copy of these poems in the poet's hands. After his death, Tsvetaeva got this account of what happened subsequently, from the woman she firmly believed to have borne his son, Nadezhda Aleksandrovna Nolle-Kogan:

> After each appearance he would receive, that same evening, heaps of letters—from women, of course. And I would always read them to him, I opened them myself, he made no objection. (And I was so jealous! Jealous of *each* single one!) He just looked on and smiled. That's how it went that evening. 'Now, where shall I begin?' Him: 'Start anywhere.' And he handed me one— it turned out to be yours—in a pale blue envelope. I opened it and started reading, but your handwriting is so particular, it was easy to start off with, then... And they were poems, I wasn't expecting that... With great seriousness, he took the pages out of my hands:
> 'No, I must read these myself.'
> He read in silence—for a long time—then such a long drawn out smile.
> He smiled so rarely, when the end came—never.

Tsvetaeva published a separate book of *Poems to Blok* in 1922, including a further group written after he had died.

In 1923, ten items from the second half of *Milestones* were gathered together as a cycle 'Sleeplessness' in the collection *Psyche*. They count among Tsvetaeva's most evocative and elusive pieces. Not actually present upon earth, she is dreamed of by her friends, or else has long since entered the grave, 'patient spectator of an immense dream'. When, in a letter to Ivask dated January 25th 1937, she speaks of her *pianissimo* moments, one thinks of a poem like 'Oh, how delicate and faint':

> When you talk about being deafening, you must also talk of quietness: I have certain lines so *quiet* no-one else has anything like them.

The figure of the prodigal returns in 'Shedding no pointless tears', while her debt to Decadent writing of the *fin-de-siècle* is palpable in 'A thin wing from the hooded cape'. 'God stooped, lost', once again self-accusatory, offers a further example of Tsvetaeva's heterodox redeployment and rephrasing of accepted religious tenets. Even after nearly two decades had passed, she herself was breathtaken at the metrical variety and virtuosity of *Milestones* (letter to Ivask dated April 4th 1933):

> In that very year 1916, I produced absolutely frenzied lines (and metres) which make my hair stand on end *today*.

*

The title of the collection presents a problem for translators. The word Tsvetaeva uses, *vyorst*, is an outdated measurement of distance corresponding to 1.06 kilometres, or 0.66 miles. I would be tempted to translate 'league', meaning the distance covered in one hour's walking, even if this is considerably more, around 3 miles. But there are interfering secondary meanings of 'ranking order' or 'conspiracy'. The Russian word can also indicate the wooden posts marking a *vyorst* on roads in Tsarist Russia. Simon Karlinsky translates it as *Mileposts*. In the end, I preferred to avoid David MacDuff's *Bon Voyages* and instead follow Robin Kemball, not least for fear unsuspecting readers might conclude a new, hitherto unknown collection by Tsvetaeva has been discovered.

Generally speaking, the poems in the book have regular, if innovative metres, and are in rhyme. I decided not to rhyme the English versions because this would have forced changes in meaning which risked taking me far from the sense of the original poems. Moreover, while in Russian the completion of a rhyme can bring a sense of inevitability and rightness to what is being expressed, all too often a translator's rhymes seem forced and arbitrary. The English language possesses a long, even dominant tradition of unrhymed verse. My concern was to devise formal constraints for each translation which, while not identical with those to be found in the original, had an analogous function. English offers the opportunity for a fruitful alternation between polysyllables—longer, more evocative, learned, even exotic words—and sequences of monosyllables which are colloquial in nuance, and respect the fundamentally analytic tendency of the modern language. I wanted Tsvetaeva's voice to ring forth in all its disarming, disconcerting directness and therefore sought native equivalents for terms which, imported from the Russian, risked being alienating or merely picturesque. My hope was that the variety of styles and metres in the translations could go some way towards mirroring the variety of Tsvetaeva's originals.

Tsvetaeva was fully aware of her excentric position in Russian literary life in the years before and immediately after the revolutions. A contradictory sense of being relegated to the sidelines, yet nonetheless unique and paradoxically central, emerges in a richly humorous passage from a letter to Raisa Lomonosova dated March 11th 1931:

I can remember a poster on the Moscow fences in 1920: EVENING FOR ALL POETS. ACMEISTS—SO AND SO—NEO-ACMEISTS—SO AND SO—IMAGISTS— SO AND SO, -ISTS, -ISTS, -ISTS then, at the very end, *beneath a gap*:
– and –
MARINA TSVETAEVA.
(Just like that – nothing around it!)
That's how it was and will be.

With Ivask, Tsvetaeva was more uncompromising (letter of April 4th 1933):

If I have always lived outside the riverbed of culture, that may be because it flowed THROUGH ME.

Certain readers may interpret this statement as witness to an unpardonable arrogance. Yet it rings true today. The closing decades of the 20th century allowed our perspective on Russian, and indeed on European poetry, to be adjusted so that Marina Tsvetaeva could take the central place which is hers by right.

Budapest,
January 2015

Milestones

The birds of Paradise all sing,
but we're not going to be let in…

I opened the small iron box,
took out of it the tear-like gift –
a little ring with a big pearl,
with a big pearl.

As a cat might do, I crept
onto the porch, and turned my face
towards the wind. Winds blew, birds soared,
swans on the left, ravens the right…
Our paths lead us two different ways.

You'll leave with the first clouds, your path
through quivering forests, over
                              burning sands.

Calling your soul out,
crying your eyes out.

While over me an owl will call,
while over me the grass will sough.

Moscow, January 1916

I planted a young apple tree,
joy and mischief for a child,
his young years in an old man's eyes,
a delight for the gardener.

I lured into my little room
a turtle dove of purest white:
the thief has nothing left to steal,
the housewife's days are sweeter now.

I gave a daughter to the world –
little eyes of brightest blue,
the same voice as a turtle dove,
hair as brilliant as the sun.
Young women had better beware,
young men had better beware too.

January 23rd 1916

I went out to the lake. Its banks were steep,
the water grey, churned up with falling snow.
Roaring jaws and deafening howls
just like from beasts.

I threw my ring away. Farewell!
Not forged to fit this hand of mine!
Gold, sink beneath the silvery foam,
sink with a song.

A brilliant arc, and then a splash!
Matched by the arc of a young swan –
see how, alarmed, it darts up high
in the grey light!

February 6th 1916

No-one went off with anything!
It suits me we should be apart.
Across hundreds of miles lying
between us, take this kiss from me.

I know our gifts are not alike.
I've never fallen dumb before.
Young Keats, what could you possibly
learn from my amateurish lines?

We meet in terrifying flight:
fledgling eagle, fly further! You
look at the sun and never blink –
is my young gaze so hard to bear?

No-one has ever watched you leave
more gently, irrevocably…
Across hundreds of years lying
between us, take this kiss from me.

February 12th 1916

Seeing off the ones I love
I sing them songs I know by heart,
It's the only way I have
of returning their gifts to me.

Along a path covered in green
we reach the point where two roads cross.
Wind, don't tire of singing to them!
Road, be soft beneath their tread!

The clouds are grey, no time for tears,
they're shod as for a holiday!
Serpent, bite your stinging tongue,
robber, put your knife away.

Should a beauty cross their path,
make your time with them a joy,
let your lips do my lips' work –
God in heaven will reward you!

Bonfires, blaze amidst the trees
so the beasts won't leave their dens.
God's Mother in heaven above,
watch over my travellers!

February 17th 1916

You throw your head back when you laugh –
you fancy yourself, chatterbox!
This February came up with quite
a joker for my company!

Ragamuffins on the run,
relishing each cigarette,
like two rampaging foreigners
we roam the place where I grew up.

No point in asking whose the hands
fondling your irresistible
eyelashes were, past what blackthorn
thickets your poet's odyssey

had you trailing. My hungry soul's
already mistress of my dream.
Divine stripling, seen through my eyes,
you could be all of ten years old.

We linger by the river rinsing
multi-coloured streetlamp beads,
I show you how to reach the square
where infant emperors were crowned…

Whistle your callow pains away,
scrunch your heart up in your fingers…
Apprentice freedman, cold-blooded and
frenzied, don't blame me for this!

February 18th 1916

What can it be disarms me so?
This isn't the first time my hands
have smoothed curls, and I've come across
lips that were darker still than yours.

The stars emerged, faded away –
what can it be disarms me so? –
your eyes emerged, faded away
into these very eyes of mine.

But I've never heard odes before
like these, intoned in darkest night,
garlanded with tenderness,
enfolded in the singer's arms.

What can it be disarms me so,
what should I do now, mischievous
scamp, poet off the train, with those
exceedingly long eyelashes?

February 18th 1916

The mirror shattered into silver
fragments, with the eyes it held.
My swans, my swans are flying home
today, are flying home!

Down from the clouds on high a feather
landed right between my arms.
Last night in a dream I scattered
small coins of silver all around.

A bell calls with a silver voice.
Singing for me's a silver thing.
Baby swan, my fosterling,
is flying what you like to do?

Without a word to mother or
to brothers I make my way to
the church, stand there and offer up
prayers to the interceding saints
for the young swan that's in my care.

March 1st 1916

Snow takes more than a day to melt.
You lie alone beneath a huge
fur coat, you're to be pitied, your
lips parched for all eternity.

Your steps are leaden, you can barely
sip, passers-by rush to get
away from you. Rogozhin gripped
a garden knife in hands like yours…

The eyes that gaze out from your face –
charred circles past their sell-by date!
Your girlfriend brought you, still a child,
to an unhappy home.

A cane knocks asphalt in the dark,
far off, the wind sets doors agape…
Be welcome, guest nobody wants,
in my brightly lit room.

March 4th 1916

Silver doves, scattering, soar in the evening sky…
All my motherly solicitude
focuses on you, my pitiful
baby raven.

Black veined with blue, blue
veined with black, your feathers,
tough, greedy, ardent
plumage.

Two others shared
your colouring – black thunderbolts effaced them! –
Lermontov and Bonaparte.

I release you into the sky,
fly on your way, pitiful creature!
Above your head,
humble and blessed,
silver doves soar, silver.

March 12th 1916

Never stop making up
songs about my cross.
Never tire of kissing
the rings on my fingers.

Things got so bad with me
no winter thunder pealed,
beasts were moved to pity,
dumb folk learned to speak.

Midnight – sun burning my skin!
Midday – stars shining on me!
My enviable wretchedness
closed over my head like waves.

For me the dead rose from the dust!
I faced the Lord on Judgement Day!
While bells chime, archangels will lead
me to the executioner's block.

March 16th 1916

Before autumn, no giddy wind
        stripped the vines bare.
Before autumn, a guest arrived
        to do the job.

I took you for a wanderer
        from Paradise.
I'm wandering too. You whispered me
        uncanny words,

and led me up a flight of steps,
        bluer than blue.
Beneath a moon bluer than blue,
        my lips took fire.

Which spring ought I to rinse them in?
        Say, pagan priest!
Take from my head the crushing wreath
        of faithfulness!

March 16th 1916

Ruined by a woman. Look,
it's written on your palm, young man!
Eyes to the ground! Keep praying! Watch your step!
The evil one's awake all night.

Heaven's gift of singing cannot keep
you safe, or those arrogant, chiselled lips.
Heaven's gift means
you're a target.

That way you have of throwing your head back,
so that the eyes, half shut, cannot be seen!
No fear, you'll get another chance
to throw it back.

Bare hands will carry you – ardent, stubborn!
You'll shout the whole night through, till the bell tolls!
They'll scatter your wings to the compass points.
Seraph! Young eagle!

March 17th 1916

The strangest malady took hold of him,
leaving him exquisitely dumbfounded.
All he can do is stand and look on high;
his child's gaze is unwavering, yet it
fails to register stars, twilight or dawn.

As he slips into sleep, eagles descend
with raucous cries, their wings tumultuous,
to fight for him incomprehensibly.
One of them – the monarch of the cliff –
uses his beak to ruffle the boy's curls.

But now his drowsy eyelids are shut tight
as, with half-parted lips, he falls asleep.
He doesn't hearken to his night-time guests,
he doesn't notice how the bird with golden
eyes is busy honing its sharp beak.

March 20th 1916

My canopies are covered with
the shadows of doves flying past.
Foster caring never ends!
Overwhelming!

I go out on the steps, the wind
blows, I lift my face, it's warm.
And yet my soul is growing numb,
immune to pity.

I linger on the topmost step,
twigs flapping all around my head.
Soon dusk will gather on the dome
of that church there.

Easter comes in a wash of clouds,
Easter comes in a wash of bells.
The first Easter on which someone's
been crucified.

March 22nd 1916

I go out to the porch and listen,
use lead to read the future – cry.
The nights are tedious,
suffocating.
Distant fires where Cossacks live.

Suburbs are no lovelier at noon:
wagons trundle across a bridge,
the beggar wants his farthing,
rapscallions chase a cat,
grasshoppers lark it up.

At evening, wrapped in a black shawl
to which I've pinned an outsize rose,
I and a scamp with rosy
cheeks and reddish curls
talk about falling out of love.

Don't think gifts of silver tempt me,
that big pearl which was your mother's
or the ring on your small finger.
What I want's much costlier,
skies aflame above the camp!

March 23rd 1916

On Annunciation day
arms are thrown open wide,
wilting flowers are watered,
windows are thrown open, for
today's my holiday!

On Annunciation day
I can make a festive declaration!
No need for tame doves, swans, young eagles!
– Fly as far as eyes can see,
today's my holiday!

On Annunciation day
I can't stop smiling till night falls
and I take leave of my winged guests.
– There isn't anything I need,
today's my holiday!

March 22nd 1916

Tomorrow's the Annunciation
and the church which bears this name
is splendidly illuminated.
Above the biggest dome,
right beneath the moon,
the stars remind one of
Constantinople.

By the grey church porch
old women stand in lines
begging for charity
in harrowing voices,
while all around God's mother
little lamps are burning
like enormous beads.

Saints' faces shine on a
sleepless, dark-haired woman
while, in the dark dome,
ice covers the small windows.
Like a golden bush
or a family tree,
the candelabra nods.
- Blessed is the fruit
of thy womb, darling
Virgin!

A candle has begun
wandering from hand to hand,
words, too, have begun
wandering from mouth to mouth:
Mother of God.

The candle's lit now,
burning brightly.

To our mother, the sun,
lost in the shadows,
I raise my voice
too, overjoyed:
Mother, protect
a mother's
dove-eyed daughter!
Enlighten her, guide her
where she has lost her way –
gracious one.

Give her good health,
at her bed's head
set an angel whose wings
carried it there from me.
Keep her safe from gorgeous language,
so people won't take her for
a bird of prey, a witch, like me.

The service is over.
No clouds in the sky.
Fervently crossing
themselves, people scatter.
Some heading homewards,
some others, nowhere,
God alone knows where
they, anyone goes!

A group of ageing
grey-haired women
lingers by the door,
crossing themselves
where little lamps
gleam just like jewels.

I cut my joyful way
through people as
through eddying waves,
hurry to Moscow's river
to see the ice pass by.

24th-25th March 1916

In your fourth year.
Eyes like ice.
Eyebrows that strike chill
already. From the Kremlin's
battlements today
you watch, for the first time,
the ice float past.

Ice floes, ice floes
and domes.
Chiming of gold,
chiming of silver.
Your arms are folded,
your lips sealed.
With raised eyebrows – Napoleon! –
you scrutinise the Kremlin.

'Mummy, where does the snow go?'
'My baby swan, it's moving on.
Past palaces, churches and gates –
on and on, my little swan!'

Her clear
blue eyes cloud over. 'Do
you love me, Mummy?'
'Lots.'
'For ever?'
'Yes.'

Soon night will fall,
we must go back:
you to the nursery, and me
to read insolent letters,
bite my lips…

The ice
keeps mov-
ing on.

March 24th 1916

Checking the girls, so in the jug the kvass
won't curdle, so the fritters won't get cold;
counting up rings, decanting aniseed
liqueur into bottles with narrow throats,

straightening out the old woman's tow thread,
smoking gum benjamin to make the house
smell good, parading the cathedral square
in rustling silks, upon godfather's arm.

Carrying a plump rooster in her apron –
her married woman's headdress black as night! –
the wet-nurse tells, in a primeval whisper,
what a young corpse they've laid out in the chapel…

Fragrant clouds have gathered in the corners,
gloomy as the vestments worn in church,
the apple-trees in blossom, white as angels,
have pigeons perched on them, grey-blue as incense.

A woman pilgrim, sipping kvass out of
the tea-kettle, sits at the very edge
of the stove bench, getting into her tale
of how a Persian beauty bewitched Razin.

March 26th 1916

Dimitry! Marina! In all the world
no fates, or names are to be found
dovetailing better than yours do,
lifted on a single wave,
swept away by a single wave!

Above your shadowy cradle,
Dimitry and, Marina
Mnishek, above your
gorgeous cradle, hung
the same ambiguous star.

It stood above your bed,
it stood above your throne
– as if planted right there –
for almost a whole year.

Dimitry, did you really have
the same birthmark on your dark cheek,
the same little black pea
his laughing mother kissed
on the true son's swarthy,
rounded cheek, the son
the emperor had fathered?
Can we take for truth
what our grandfathers always said,
that we cannot judge sinners?

A necklace on the child's
long, vulnerable neck.
A dazzling bright garland
adorns his shining hair.

In Martha's dark cell
a glittering necklace
burns – sun in the night!

Her eyes, remembering,
devoured him - people gaped.
Her lips, remembering,
devoured his mouth – but whose?

She was a nun,
but knew her child!
How could we think it wasn't you?

Marina! Emperor's wife,
star of the pretender!
It's you I sing,
your evil beauty,
cheeks never red.
Praising you I'm guilty of
excessive pride, the emperors' sin.
I bear with honour
your honoured name.

Lodestar to my tempests,
Marina – Yury's daughter,
sun amidst the stars.

She removed her golden cross,
then took down the black casket,
greased the key with holy grease
so it shifted easily.
The sorceress extracted her
black book of evil spells.

The truth is, it was late:
the angel had already
left her shoulders – gone
to bring her lord bad news.

– Bad news, my lord and master!
A smooth-tongued thief has ruined her!

Marina! Dimitry! Rebels,
darlings, sleep in peace.
On the beloved tomb an angel guards
in the Cathedral of the Archangel,
an outsize candle burns for you.

29th, 30th March 1916

Poems about Moscow

1

Clouds all around,
domes all around,
hands over Moscow –
room for so many! –
I carry you, most precious weight,
my little sapling
weighing nothing.

Through this city of wonders,
through this city of peace
where even after death
I shall be filled with joy –
you have to reign, to grieve,
to let them garland you,
firstborn of mine!

Fasting and prayer,
unblackened brow,
honouring forty
times forty churches,
pilgrim on foot – light, youthful step!
exploring all
its seven hills.

Your time will come
to give your daughter
Moscow too
with tender pain…
For me, my fill of sleep, ringing of bells,
dawns breaking on the graves
of Vagankovo.

March 31st 1916

2

Take from my hands a city no hands built,
my idiosyncratic, comely brother,

its churches, one by one – forty times forty –
together with the doves that soar above,

the Saviour's Gate that flowers decorate,
where every true believer doffs his cap,

the star-filled chapel, refuge from all ills,
in which kisses have worn the floor away.

Take its matchless ring of five cathedrals,
inspired friend, redolent of ancient times.

I'll lead my foreign guest into the garden
to Our Lady of Unexpected Joy,

the pure gold church domes will be glittering bright,
the pealing out of belltowers will not sleep

and God's mother will let her cloak fall down
out of the purple clouds to cover you.

Then you'll arise, replete with wondrous strength,
not sorry that you fell in love with me.

March 31st 1916

3

Squares rush us at top speed
past nocturnal towers.
How scary in the dark
shouting from young soldiers!

Peal forth, thunder-filled heart!
Kiss more ardently, love!
Shouting like animals!
Such impertinent blood!

My mouth's scorched, it's no help
my gaze being like a saint's.
The Georgian Virgin burns
like a casket of gold.

Put your mischief aside
and light a candle so
this night won't end for us
the way I want it to.

March 31st 1916

4

One day – people maintain, a sad one – they'll
stop giving laws, burning hot, shedding tears;
a coin from a strange country will cool both
these eyes of mine, which moved restless as flames;
a face, groping its way towards its double,
will coalesce beyond transparent features.
At last I'll reach the stage where I deserve you,
priceless belt girding the sacred image!

Along a black path in the distance – do
I glimpse you in their midst? – crossing themselves,
a crowd of anxious pilgrims will approach,
seeking this hand of mine I won't refuse,
seeking this hand to which nothing's forbidden,
seeking this hand, which no longer exists.

You who still live, to start with I won't raise
any objections to being kissed by you.
The sacred image's exquisite cloak
will clothe me from the head right to the toes.
Nothing will bring a red flush to my cheeks
as I celebrate holy Eastertide.

Along the streets of an abandoned Moscow
I'll make my way, and there you, too, will plod,
neither of us lagging as the first
clod clatters down onto the coffin's lid;
I shall finally be released from this
self-involved and solitary dream.
From now on there'll be nothing more Marina,
the late lamented noblewoman, needs.

April 11th 1916, First day of Easter

5

Across the city which Peter rejected
pealing out of belltowers roars like thunder.

Frothy, thundering wavetops close above
the head of a woman whom you rejected.

All I can do is thank both emperors,
Peter and you. The bells, though, are still higher.

As long as they thunder from a blue sky,
Moscow's primacy is uncontested.

And all of its forty times forty churches
greet emperors' impudence with peals of laughter!

May 28th 1916

6

Over the blue haze of the woods round Moscow
a rain of pealing bells falls in a drizzle.
Down the Kaluga road, so exquisite

and rich in song, blind men are shuffling, while
the rain of bells wipes out the humble names
of pilgrims in the darkness singing hymns.

I realise that, before much time goes by,
tired of you all, my enemies, my friends,
tired of the pliancy of Russian speech,

I'll hang a cross of silver round my neck,
and, crossing myself, make off silently
along the old road leading to Kaluga.

Feast of the Trinity 1916

7

Seven hills resembling seven bells!
A steeple for each of the seven bells!
The sum of churches is forty times forty.
Seven hills studded with pealing steeples!

One day of scarlet, in the bell-filled city,
feast of John the Evangelist, I came
into the world, in a gingerbread house,
round it a wattle fence, churches, gold domes.

When the first bell sounded, I fell in love
with nuns proceeding on their way to mass,
with roaring ovens, overwhelming sleep
and the quack doctor in the house next door.

Be my escort, all of Moscow's rabble,
you, robbers, flagellants and inspired fools!
Priest, you can't stuff too much of Moscow's earth
into my mouth, all filled with ringing bells!

July 8th 1916, Feast of the Kazan Virgin

8

Moscow! Enormous city
so welcoming to strangers!
All of us in old Russia
are homeless. You're our home.

Shamefully branded shoulders,
knife tucked inside a boot,
you summon all of us,
no matter how far off.

The brand a convict bears,
sickness of every kind,
infant St Panteleimon
can heal all of us.

Just beyond those doors
people are thronging to,
the Georgian Virgin's heart
gleams in a pure gold frame.

Hallelujahs flood
onto the twilit fields.
Earth sustaining Moscow,
I kiss you on the heart!

July 8th 1916, Feast of the Kazan Virgin

9

The rowan tree flared
in a cluster of red.
Trees were shedding their leaves.
I came into the world.

Hundreds of church bells
engaged in dispute.
It was Saturday, John
the Evangelist's day.

I feel even now
the same urge to chew
bright, bitter berries
from the rowan tree.

August 16th 1916

Bent over double from sheer badness,
a crazed old hag had this to say to me:
You're not the one to rock a child to sleep,
no-one will catch you bleaching woven cloth –
you'll be dictating law beneath the fences!
Better save up your kisses for a raven!

I went pale as a cloud high in the sky:
Go and fetch the white blouse from the drawer,
no need to find a steed to pull my hearse,
no need to fetch a priest from the cathedral.
Bury me underneath an apple tree,
without reciting prayers or kindling incense.

In sign of thanks for your advice, for all
the sovereign favours showered on me, such as,
your pockets never anything but empty,
the prison songs I learned from you, your blend
of infamy and mutiny, the cruel
way you loved me, see, I bow down deeply.

When the bells toll there in the cathedral,
devils will turn up to haul me off.
So that God can hear me, I'm repeating
what I said the day the two of us
raised our glasses, lad: I loved you more
than my good name, more than the light of day.

April 1st 1916

Seeing his scattered locks,
golden and leonine,
seeing that belt he's got,
the way he puts one foot
after the other, who
wouldn't run after him,
that whistle and that belt,
all through the daylight world!

When I walk down the street
people move to one side,
she's a robber, they say,
she's a ghost, and she haunts!
No-one's left in the dark
what sort of gods are mine,
which little chapels, decked
out in green, I pray in.

Well, girls, I've only got
myself to blame for this,
don't look for pigeon's down
to weave a shroud for me.

I never slept alone,
so, for eternal sleep,
no incense – bury me
by a wild apple tree.

April 2nd 1916 (Palm Sunday)

Drink and eat, be of good cheer!
And yet a day must come
on which they'll lay my body at
the place where four roads meet,

a haunt for ravens and for wolves,
amidst deserted fields.
Erect a cross over my head,
the kind that marks crossroads!

At night I didn't keep away
from places that were cursed.
Lift yourself high over me,
cross without a name.

Friends, not one of you could eat
or drink enough of me.
Now it's time for country weeds
to grow above my head!

Light no candles for my sake
in the murky church.
I'd rather be forgotten in
the land where I was born.

April 4th 1916

Roads go in all directions,
through wastelands and through forests,
from morning until late.

People walking along them,
carts trundling along them
from morning until late.

Soles of pilgrims' feet
trampling sand and clay,
trampling flint and mud...

Battling the wind – a cripple?
Everyone on the highroad
can be a disguised prince.

Tattered garments flapping
wherever skies are blue,
wherever God is judge.

The twin ruts of the road
make their fetters collide,
their tatters intermingle.

And so, across earth's wastelands,
forgetting hunky dory,
avoiding settled places,

royal children begging,
princesses and princes
sentenced to hard labour.

See how roads come together,
we bumped into each other.
The hour couldn't be darker.

This isn't me and you –
one misery confronts
another – both are convicts.

Give me a kiss then, darling,
here on the lips, since God
couldn't save you from me.

We'll all of us be lugged
down one road on our hearses,
in the morning, or late.

April 5th 1916

My soul's a tempting bait, they give me tender
names enough for a saints' calendar.

Talk about godfathers and christenings –
I've got enough to fill a monastery!

Even priests find me irresistible!
Not a day but I turn up at the font!

His baby eagle, or his little goldfinch,
everyone finds a new name for me.

There's no law in the book I haven't broken,
yet men and women leap to my defence!

Laying my body out, they'll put my tender
calendar of saints' names next to it.

OK, so each one used a different nickname –
all of them called me, no-one got it right.

April 6th 1916

As long as you're with me, you won't get bored!
What they call me's the Virgin with Three Hands:
one shatters fortresses, the second does
the same, the third writes letters on the waves

for the fishes to read. But if a bungler
shows up, no-one will credit what they see.
What sort of a nun's this? Owls hooting, cats'
backs arched – a sorceress they won't forget!

I don't crawl on my belly, I like riding!
Should I walk with my mirror on black ice?
To meet your lordly needs, I could sweep chimneys!
Just don't ask me to fuss over a baby!

Think I'm somebody's wife? Then where's my headscarf?
If I'm a widow, where's my husband buried?
Waiting for Mr Right? I sleep too well!
Empress and Maiden – I'm beyond the law!

April 6th 1916

Sleeplessness has traced a shadow ring
around my eyes.
Sleeplessness has weaved a shadow garland
round my eyes.

What's this, then? They're forbidden,
night-time prayers to idols!
Your secret wasn't safe with me,
idol worshipper.

Not enough for you,
the day, not the sun's fire!

Pallid-faced one, wear
a ring or two of mine.
You cried aloud, inflicted
a garland made from shadow.

Not called my name enough?
Want to sleep more with me?

There you lie, face untroubled.
People bow to you.
Sleeplessness, I'll be
the one who reads to you.

Sleep, now you are calm,
now you have your reward,
sleep, woman, now you've got
a garland for your head.

I'll sing you a song
to help you drop off:

Sleep, little darling one
victim to restlessness,
sleep, little jewel of mine,
sleeplessness, sleep.

Was there anyone we wrote
no letters, swore no oaths to?
Fall asleep.

See, the inseparable
finally separate.
See how your little hands
slip out of mine.

Dearest of martyrs, an
end to your torments.

Holy – sleep.
They all – sleep.
Garland – off.

April 8th 1916

You could have been my mother in those days.
Feverish, insomniac light, I could
call on you from nightfall until dawn,
you were the light of my eyes in those days.

Look back upon them, you so rich in gifts,
those days on which the sun would never set,
days on which we played mother and daughter,
days when no sunset came, no evening fell.

Please, I haven't come to trouble you,
I only want to kiss your dress's hem,
I want my eyes to look straight into yours,
the ones I kissed so often on those nights.

Some day I'll die, and some day you will, too,
some day I'll understand, you'll do the same…
Those days are irretrievable, but when
forgiving's feasible, we'll get them back.

April 26th 1916

I came to you at dead of night
as my last hope of help,
a mendicant, her origins
unknown, a sinking ship.

In my fiefs interregnum reigns,
monks hatch their plots, while dog-
keepers wield power, and anyone
can don the emperor's robes.

Who didn't fight over my lands
or get my guards drunk? Who
didn't boil up their slops at night,
set the skyline in flames?

Upstarts and rapacious dogs
robbed everything I had.
I stand outside your palace door
begging, true emperor!

April 27th 1916

Roll up! Roll up! Roll up!
No time to waste, good people!
I've got priceless stock to sell,
clean things nobody has worn
or fiddled with, it all wears well –
at prices beggaring belief!

Stock to suit all styles, all tastes.
Halt there, pedlars with your trays!
The prices I ask aren't outlandish.
You decide how much it's worth!
Try it – you won't take it off!
You'll never throw these clothes away!

Nobody else has stock like mine!
Let's see those bright coppers of yours!
And pray for my soul once I'm gone!

April 28th 1916

Poems to Blok

1

Your name's a bird caught in the hand,
your name's an ice-cube on the tongue,
the merest movement of two lips,
four letters go to make your name.
A ball caught as it's flying past,
small bell of silver in the mouth,

stone tossed into a silent pool –
the name they call you sobs like that.
Your name's a peal of thunder in
the soft clatter of night-time hooves,
a trigger clicking at the temple
has the resonance of your name.

Your name – but I'm breaking the rules! –
is when you get kissed on the eyes,
on gentle, chill, unmoving lids –
your name's somebody kissing snow.
Spring water gulped, ice-cold and blue…
Your name's a talisman for sleep.

April 15th 1916

2

Kindly phantom,
knight beyond reproach,
who told you you could enter
my young life?

Midst grey-blue fog,
you stand, decked out
in snow-white vestments.

It's not some wind that sends me
running through the city:
for three evenings now
I've sensed a hostile presence.

A singer of snow
has bewitched me with
his blue evil eye.

A snow-white swan scatters
feathers before me
which flutter, then slowly
dissolve in the snow.

As if across feathers,
I go to a door
behind which stands – death.

Beyond azure panes
he sings me his song,
he sings it in bells
chiming far off,

his protracted cry,
his swan song
summoning me.

Benevolent phantom!
I know I'm dreaming.
Have mercy on me!
Amen, amen, dissolve!
Amen.

May 1st 1916

3

You take your way past with the setting sun,
you'll look upon the world when twilight comes,
you take your way past with the setting sun,
the whirling snow obliterates your steps.

Passionless, you take your way beyond
my windows, in a silence filled with snow,
fine-featured, righteous in the eyes of God,
you, silent luminary of my soul.

I harbour no designs upon your soul!
The path you follow is inviolate.
No-one will catch me hammering my nail
into a hand whose colour kisses drained.

It's not my plan to call you by your name
or stretch either of my hands out towards you.
All I shall do is bow from far away
towards a waxen, consecrated face.

As the white flakes unhurriedly descend,
I'll fall upon my knees amidst the snow
and, in homage to your holy name,
place a kiss amidst the evening snow

where, your paces filled with majesty,
you strode into the silence of the grave,
silent luminary, holy glory,
undisputed ruler of my soul.

4

A beast needs its lair,
a pilgrim the road,
the dead need a hearse.
Let each have what's his.

Women need to cheat
and emperors to rule.
All I need's to sing
praises of your name.

May 2nd 1916

5

Here in my Moscow – domes burning bright!
Here in my Moscow – pealing of bells!
Where I live, lined up in their graves,
emperors sleep, and empresses.

You don't realise, when dawn breaks on the Kremlin,
one breathes the freest anywhere on earth!
You don't realise, when dawn breaks on the Kremlin,
I start worshipping you – until night falls!

Just when you take your constitutional
beside the Neva, here by Moscow's river
I stand and let my head droop – as the light
from one streetlamp gets glued onto the next.

With all my inability to sleep
I love you, my ears hearken to you while,
from one end to the other of the Kremlin,
bell-ringers are awakening from sleep…

And all the same, it's not my river's fate
to meet with yours, my hand's to hold your hand,
delight of mine, until dawn finally
reaches the point at which the sky grows dark.

May 7th 1916

6

Concluding that he must be human,
they permitted him to die.
He won't come back to life again.
– Shed your tears for the dead angel!

At the sunset hour he sang
praises of the evening's beauty.
Waxen and untrustworthy,
three candles were flickering.

Meanwhile he emitted rays –
burning streamlets on the snow!
Three candles of purest wax –
for our sun, brilliant, serene!

All of you, see how his lids have
sunk inside their darkened sockets!
All of you, see how his wings are
straggling now they're snapped in two!

Chanting of black litanies,
idle hands that form a cross…
Laid out on his bier, the singer
celebrates return to life.

May 9th 1916

7

The village where I used to live
has to lie beyond those trees.
Love has to be easier
and simpler than I used to think.

Idols, time to croak your last!
Rising, he produced a whip:
a peremptory shout, then lashes,
a renewed tinkling of bells.

Above the waving, wretched corn
pole lifts itself high after pole
while, beneath the sky, the wires
sing unceasingly of death.

May 13th 1916

8

Gadflies swarm around indifferent jades,
the wind swells red calico from Kaluga,
whistling quails, immeasurable skies,
a sea of bells breaks on a sea of corn,
talk of the Germans till it's nauseous,
a yellow cross beyond the bluish grove,
hot but not too hot, radiance overhead,
your name that so resembles the word "angel".

May 18th 1916

I adore kissing
hands, adore
giving out names
and then throwing
doors
wide open on dark night!

Head in my hands,
hearing a weighty tread
grow lighter somewhere
while the wind sets the sleepy,
sleepless forest
rocking.

Night! Night!
Springs bubbling somewhere
make me drowsy.
I almost sleep.
Somewhere in the night
somebody's drowning.

May 27th 1916

Poems to Akhmatova

1

Muse of weeping, loveliest of the muses!
Maddened demon of the shortest night,
unleashing a black snowstorm on your country,
your howls, like arrows, cut into our flesh.

And we all flinch, emit a suppressed moan,
on which a hundred thousand swear by Anna
Akhmatova! The name, an immense sigh,
precipitates into a nameless chasm.

The crown we bear is treading the same earth,
walking beneath the same heavens as you!
Whoever's wounded by your mortal fate
is deathless when laid out upon his bier.

Church domes burn brightly in my song-filled city,
blind beggars praise the feastday of our Saviour…
Here, take the gift, Akhmatova, of my
bell-ringing city, with my heart as bonus.

June 19th 1916

2

Head held between my hands, I stand –
men's intrigues pale! –
head held between my hands, I sing
as twilight falls.

A furious wave has lifted me
high on its crest!
I sing you, peerless in our midst,
moon in the sky!

Seizing, as ravens do, a heart
you lift skywards,
hook-nosed, your rage as killing as
your clemency.

Stretching darkness out over my
pure gold Kremlin,
your tender singing throttles me,
a tightening belt.

I'm lucky! Never will a dawn
burn more clearly.
I'm lucky! Bringing you this gift
makes me a beggar.

For I was first – abysses! fogs! –
although your voice
cut my breath short, to christen you
Tsar's Village muse.

June 22nd 1916

3

One further immense sweep, and then
lashes close tight.
Flesh infinitely dear! Dust too
light for a bird.

Her business in the fog of days?
To wait, to sing…
She had so little flesh on her,
such ample breath.

Her drowsiness endears us in
inhuman ways.
In her angel, eagle combine
some quality.

Concerted voices beckon her
to Eden's vale.
Demon that has dozed off, not tired
of singing yet!

= = =

Hours, years and centuries. Not meant
for us, or our
abodes. The monument takes root,
starts to forget.

It's ages since a broom swept here.
And, teasingly,
above Tsar's Village muse, crosses
of nettle nod.

23rd June 1916

4

The boy's called Leo,
his mother Anna.
In his name, anger,
quiet in hers.
He's ginger-haired –
head like a tulip!
Who cares? Hats off!
An emperor's son.

May God give him
his mother's breathing,
her smile, and a
pearl-diver's eyes.
God, keep an eye
on him. An emperor's
son's enigmatic,
not like the rest.

Ginger-haired whelp
with the green eyes
and an appalling legacy!

Grasping oceans
to north and south
and a black rosary's threaded pearls!

June 24th 1916

5

So many followers and friends!
You echo none.
Suffering and pride keep those
young years in check.

Recall the harbour, a wild day,
threatening south winds,
the Caspian's roar – a rose's stem
between your lips.

The stone a gypsy woman gave,
carved round the rim,
the mumbled prophecy she made
of coming fame.

High up among the sails, a lad
in a blue shirt.
Waves roaring, and a wounded muse's
awful cry.

July 25th 1916

6

I won't be left behind! You are the guard,
I'm the convict. We share a single fate,
one and the same relay of horses has
to serve us both, amidst these empty wastes.

Just look at me! Already grown so calm!
Look in my eyes and see how bright they are!
Take pity on me, guard, and give me leave
to wander toward the clump of pine-trees there!

July 26th 1916

7

You, who tear the covers off
from cradles and from catafalques,
who rouse the winds to fury and
send snowstorms blasting down on us,

recurrent fevers, verses, wars –
black sorceress! Oppressor of serfs! –
I heard how terrifyingly
the lions of your chariot roar,

I hear impassioned voices cry
while one voice stubbornly stays mute,
I see red sails spread open, in
their midst a single sail that's black.

Whether your way leads you across
the ocean, or else through the air,
arms open wide as to the sun,
I wait to be condemned to die.

July 26th 1916

8

People were shouting at the fair,
smoke billowed from the baker's stall.
I can remember the street singer's
crimson lips, and her drawn face.

In a dark, flower-patterned shawl –
God's mother take pity on us! –
you stood, eyes downcast, with the women
pilgrims at St Sergey's and

the Trinity. Heartbroken and
demonic beauty, pray for me
when, in the forests, you are named
Madonna of the Flagellants.

July 27th 1916

9

Anna Chrysostom of the Golden Lips
(murmuring that name, the whole of Russia's ransomed) –
transport my voice, wind, till it reaches her,
make sure my heavy sighs travel that far.

Skyline beset with flames, ensure she learns
how suffering has darkened these eyes of mine,
tell her that somewhere, in the golden grain,
I bow down to the earth, without a sound.

Returning back where you belong
amidst the thundering heights,
you for whom I can find no name,
bear golden-lipped Anna my love,
patron of this whole land!

July 27th 1916

10

A voice today in the thin wire above
the rippling oats is like a thousand voices!

And, Lord, the passing bells' voice is the same
as they proclaim her: Holy, holy, holy.

I stand and hearken, chew an ear of corn;
the voice encloses me, a darkening dome.

= = =

It's not these willow twigs as they float past
I touch so reverently, but your hands.

Earthly woman for all who nearly faint,
hailing your coming – heavenly cross for me!

To you alone, when night comes, do I bend
my knee, and all the icons have *your* eyes!

July 1st 1916

11

You catch hold of my sun high in
the sky, your fist holds all the stars!
If only – doors thrown open wide! –
I could go in you like the wind!

Start babbling, the next thing flare up,
all of a sudden lower my eyes,
burst into tears, fall silent as
a child who gets forgiven does.

July 2nd 1916

They gave me hands to stretch towards everyone
unstintingly, lips for bestowing names,
eyes for not seeing, brows to arch gently in
surprise at love, more gently at its absence.

A bell, too, heavier than all the Kremlin's,
pealing repeatedly from deep within…
Who's to say? Can it be? Maybe, for certain –
I cannot be a guest on Russian soil!

July 2nd 1916

The sun's bleached pale. The clouds are low. Behind
a white wall by the vegetable plots,
the village graveyard. Scarecrows made of straw,
as tall as men, with crosspole arms, line up

in sandy soil. I lean against a fencepost,
observe the road, the trees, the milling soldiers.
Next to the gate, an old crone scatters salt
across her black bread crust, chews it morosely.

What have these drab huts done to make you angry,
God? Why pierce so many with your arrows?
A hooting train passes, the soldiers hoot,
dust lifts in clouds on the departing road.

I want to die! Better not to be born
than listen to this sad, pathetic, howling
prison-camp song of beauties with black brows
which the soldiers take up. Good God in heaven!

July 3rd 1916

In this immense city of mine – night.
From a sleep-filled house I sally – forth.
People see me and think – daughter, wife.
But in my head there's only room for – night.

The path I take a July wind sweeps – clear.
Music from a window – phantom trace.
Till day breaks, all the wind can do is – blow
from one rib cage into another – cage.

A darkening poplar, in a window – light,
a bell-tower ringing, in my hand – a flower,
this step of mine pursuing – nobody,
my shadow's moving, but there's not a – me.

Fires – like gold beads strung along a thread,
in my mouth the taste of a night leaf.
Friends, release me from the lips of day,
remember that you're only dreaming – me.

July 17th 1916
Moscow

After a night without sleep the whole body is weaker,
tenderer somehow, belonging to somebody else.
Pricking of arrows in veins where the blood flows so slowly –
you could be an angel, you hand smiles out left, right and centre.

After a night without sleep, the arms, too, grow weaker,
you couldn't care less who your enemy is, who your friend.
The most casual sound has a rainbow's entire iridescence,
in the frost, without warning, you pick up a fragrance of Florence.

Lips become brighter and gentler, around bleary eyes
the shadow's more golden. A face of untellable brilliance
was kindled by night, and the only reminder of darkness,
the only dim thing that is left about us is – our eyes.

July 19th 1916

Now I'm a heavenly guest
in your country.
I saw the sleepless wood,
the fields asleep.

Hooves somewhere in the dark
tore at the grass.
A cow sighed deeply in
a sleepy shed.

I've got a mournful tale,
mournful, tender,
about a goose on guard,
the sleeping geese.

Hands plunged deep in a dog's
grey fur. It can't
have been much before six
when daybreak came.

July 20th 1916

Yet again,
a thin, black shadow,
she vanishes behind the postcoach door.
Night
rushes to catch up.

Black greatcoat,
black top hat and veil.
In her hands
a travelling rug with spacious checks.
If you've no taste for trouble,
neighbour – go back to sleep.

Sleepwalker's footstep. Drawn
and feverish features.
The burning eyes
are black gashes.
The scarf slips from her neck
onto her knees,
sharp elbows dig
into sharp knees.

A puny candle-end
gutters in the lantern.
The postcoach is a ship.
The postcoach is a ship.
Forest trees
thrust against the window.
Soon dawn will break.

If you've no taste for trouble,
neighbour – go back to sleep.

July 23rd 1916

A female adventurer, a man
looking for danger, once again
we're fated to come face to face
by preordained coincidence.

But an ocean separates us,
your London huddled in its fogs,
the roses at a wedding feast,
Britain's lion (valour's symbol)
retribution from the fifth
commandment – and this wind-filled lyre!

There was no place for me on earth
the last time either!
Last time, as now, my home on earth
was everywhere.

While on the family estate
a charming bride awaited you.

At night-time in the postcoach,
we clinked frothing Asti,
I made stanzas for you which
had as their subject passion's charms.

The *vetturino* cracked his whip,
the pine trees bowed in greeting – *Salve*!
Corinna's what they called me then,
as for you – your name was Oswald.

July 24th 1916

Daniel

1

I sat on the sill, dangling my legs
when he asked in a low voice: Who's that there?
– It's me. I came. – But why? – I couldn't say.

I saw the moon on high,
saw the moon and its beam
resting on your little window –
that must be why I came…

But why were you called Daniel? I can't stop
dreaming lions are tearing you apart!

July 26th 1916

2

Women on horseback, ruins, psalms,
hills that are overgrown with heather,
our meek horses ride side by side,
his chin's outline is like a lion's,
he wears a clergyman's black garb,
his gaze is shy and penetrating…

You're calling on a dying woman,
I travel on the ridge with you
(a girl, but no-one asks you questions!)
A horn call from amidst the pines…
– Interpreter of dreams, why have
your curls turned prematurely grey?

Blue-coloured glitter from the lake,
the miller's wife rolls back her sleeves,
his burning gaze turned to one side,
he talks about a wretched widow,
says all of us must love Jehovah,
I shouldn't cry the way I do…

Fragrance of apple-trees and smoke,
we're calling on a dying woman,
he says our whole world is a dream,
that my hair's like a helmet, nothing
lasts… I'm silent – on it all
Daniel the visionary smiles.

July 26th 1916

3

In the full moon the horses snorted,
a gypsy did rounds of the girls.
In the full moon, the organ started
playing alone in the red church.

The flock went crazy in the meadow,
bleating: the world is at an end!
They found the young vicar the following
morning at the organ, dead.

Tears on his silver cheeks. The whole
day long, roses kept pouring in,
an abundant tribute from
the surrounding villages.

But when the dead man found a place
in his forefathers' peaceful home,
the russet-haired girl set the four
corners of her Bible burning.

July 28th 1916

Tonight I'm alone in the night, a nun
who cannot sleep and has nowhere to go.
Tonight I have the key to every door
in this incomparable capital.

Sleeplessness set me going on my way –
how wonderful, how glimmering you are,
my Kremlin! – I can kiss the very core
of the whole round, war-waging globe tonight.

It's not my hair that's ruffling. This is fur!
A sultry wind blows right into my soul.
Tonight my heart goes out to everyone
who's pitied, and to everyone who's kissed.

August 1st 1916

Oh, how delicate and faint
the whistling is amidst the pines!
In a dream I caught a glimpse
of a child. Its eyes were black.

Dripping down the shapely tree,
see the burning resin flow
while, in my exquisite night,
a saw cuts its teeth on my heart.

August 8th 1916

Not something I can get worked up about –
what happens to the seeds.
Not me, someone enormous wanted that,
angel, lion combined.

It's dizziness I watch for in young eyes,
blackness, intensity.
My business – starting fires, from heart to heart,
from home to home.

Curls get dishevelled, collars are torn open…
Emptiness! Flight!
Clouds moving onwards, over me the burning
city, too, moves.

August 2nd 1916

Dark as a pupil, and absorbing light
as pupils do – I love you, sharp-eyed Night.

Singing's ancient mother, in your hands
the reins of the four winds, give me a voice

to summon you, one that can sing your praise -
me, shell in which the ocean murmurs on.

I'm tired of looking into human eyes!
Black sun, night, burn me, reduce me to ash!

August 9th 1916

Stooping from his troubles, God
fell silent.
Next he smiled, created
legions of holy angels
whose bodies were
resplendent.
Some have immense wings,
others none at all.

That's why I cry so much,
because –
more than with God, I fell
in love with his sweet angels.

August 15th 1916

A thin wing from the hooded cape
settled on the hand next mine.
You understood, companion in
wretchedness, that I *do* have wings!
How sad you're not able to cope
with my accursèd tenderness!

Thankful for the warmth I brought,
you place a kiss on my thin wing.

The wind puts out the makeshift fires
and sets the motley tent-flaps twitching.
It also lifts the little wing
of my cape away from your hand…
And sighs: Take good care of your soul!
And don't love women who have wings!

September 21st 1916

Shedding no pointless tears
for either of your parents, stir yourself,
set off at night-time down
the highroads - without either dog or lamp.

Night's jaws are like a thief's:
it swallows shame, separates you from God.
What's more, it can teach songs,
how to rob people, smiling in their eyes,

issue a summons with
protracted whistling where black roads meet,
or kiss beneath the trees
compliant women you've not seen before.

Whether grain floods the land
or ice, the roads bring wonder after wonder!
Only in stories does
the prodigal go back home to his father.

October 10th 1916

I kiss leaves burnished crimson and sleepy mouths,
leaves that fly and mouths that sleep. –
Nothing else interested me in the world. –
Sleep, sleeping mouths,
fly, flying leaves!

October 16th 1916

Hold on a moment, friend!
Haven't we tramped the city streets enough?
Let's find a basement bar
to while the night away.

The place for you and me,
where people kiss and drink, pour wine and tears,
voices are raised in song
and you get food and drink.

Wood's burning in the stove,
a knife gets passed from hand to swarthy hand,
there even I am right,
there even you are good.

Look at her there – darker
than darkest night, no-one sits next to her!
And the look in her eyes!
And the sound of her voice!

October 22nd 1916

If fate had wanted us to be united
what a carnival earth would have seen!
We'd have got keys to city after city,
my kin, my natural, my bastard brother!

After the last lamp on the bridge went out
we'd have dictated law throughout the taverns:
all of you, swear allegiance to my emperor,
and me, his empress – everyone can have me!

If fate had wanted us to be united,
we'd have kept the emperor's bells in work,
ringing all down Moscow's river for
the beautiful pretender and her boyfriend.

Strutting, dancing, partying crazily,
the night wind would have rocked us to and fro,
while on the road the dust blew whiter, whiter,
if fate had wanted us to be united!

October 25th 1916

Every day's a Saturday for me!
The bells begin to ring and you pop round,
looking so wonderful that, in her shrine
of gold and glass, God's mother can't help smiling.

Night after night, a stone's on top of me,
crushing my heart like the palm of a hand
and I can't move until you say, until
I hear your order: Young woman, get up!

November 8th 1916

Along paths gently resonant with frost
I and my royal child enrobed in silver
proceed. Snow, death and sleep are everywhere.

The bushes are quivers of silver arrows.
At one time I was gifted with a body.
I had a name, too. Was all that mere smoke?

I had a voice, burning and resonant…
Some people claim that child in silver ermine,
the one with eyes of palest blue, is mine…

No-one who passes by has realised
that I've been in my grave for centuries,
patient spectator of an immense dream.

November 15th 1916

Who sleeps when night falls? Nobody can sleep!
In its cradle a child calls out aloud.
An old man sits, all he can think about
his death, young men talk to the girl they love,
breathe on her lips and stare into her eyes.

You drop off – will you wake up here again?
We'll do it! Somehow we'll manage to sleep!

The keen-eyed watchman moves from house
to house, a rose-like lantern in his hand.
His unrelenting rattle clatters on,
beating out its rhythm on the pillow:
Don't sleep! Be strong! Hearken to my words!
Not this – eternal sleep, eternal home!

December 12th 1916

Look – another window
where they still can't sleep.
They might be drinking wine
or just sitting, like that,
or else one hand can't bear
to let another go.
Friend, each building has
a window that's like this.

Neither lights nor lamps kindled the darkness –
sleepless eyes did!

Window in the night, a cry
of partings and of meetings!
One hundred lights, maybe,
or else merely three candles...
No way that this mind
of mine can get peace.
– Things were just the same
when I stayed at home.

Send up a prayer, friend, for a sleepless house,
the window beyond which a fire is burning!

Moscow, December 23rd 1916

Notes

These notes complement the information already supplied in the 'Introduction', and are intended to be read in conjunction with that. In preparing them, full use has been made of the standard editions by Russica of New York and Ellis Lak of Moscow, as well of Robin Kemball's admirable bilingual edition, published by Northwestern University Press in 2003. I am grateful to Tanya Filosofova for checking the final draft against the Russian original and offering valuable feedback.

'No-one went off with anything!'
The original mentions, not Keats, but Gavril Derzhavin (1743-1816), an outstanding poet of the classical period in Russia.

'The mirror shattered into silver'
Tsvetaeva used 'young swan' as an endearment for Tikhon Churilin, the addressee of several poems at this stage in the collection.

'Snow takes more than a day to melt'
Rogozhin is a character in Dostoevsky's novel *The Idiot* (1868-69), who attempts to stab the hero Prince Myshkin, and finally murders the female protagonist, Natasha Filippovna.

'Silver doves, scattering, soar in the evening sky...'
Mikhail Yurevich Lermontov (1814-1841) was a Russian Romantic poet with distant Scottish origins. Tsvetaeva's admiration for Napoleon Bonaparte was a constant in her life.

'On Annunciation day'
On March 25th, the Feast of the Annunciation, tradition required that caged birds should be set free.

'Checking the girls, so in the jug the kvass'
Kvass is a fermented drink made from rye bread in Russia and the Ukraine. Stenka Razin headed an unsuccessful Cossack uprising in 1670-71. In 1917 Tsvetaeva wrote a series of three poems concerning the Persian beauty he was said to have abducted, then drowned in the Volga.

'Dimitry! Marina! In all the world'
See the Introduction for Dimitry the Pretender and Marina Mnishek, whose father Yury, or Jerzy, was a Polish voivode. Martha or Maria Nagaya, mother of the true Dimitry and last wife of Ivan the Terrible, claimed to recognise the false Dimitry as her son when he was shown to her.

Poems to Moscow

1   Vagankovo is a Moscow cemetery in which Tsvetaeva's parents, her maternal grandparents and her brother are buried. This poem heads the cycle 'Poems to my Daughter' in *Psyche* (1923), which includes two other items from *Milestones*, 'In your fourth year' and 'Along paths gently resonant with frost'.

2   The gate of the Spasskaya or Saviour's tower was once the principal entrance to the Kremlin. Our Lady of Unexpected Joy is a celebrated, supposedly wonder-working icon. The original of the famed icon in the Iverskaya Chapel is kept in the Georgian monastery of Iviron on Mount Athos.

6   The province of Kaluga is located around the Oka River some 100 miles south of Moscow. Tsvetaeva spent childhood summer holidays there, in the town of Tarusa.

9   The feast of St John the Evangelist or the Divine was celebrated on September 26th, Tsvetaeva's birthday, corresponding, when she was born, to October 9th in the Gregorian calendar used elsewhere in Europe.

'As long as you're with me, you won't get bored!'
The Virgin with Three Hands is another miraculous icon. St John of Damascus was said to have added a third hand when his own, severed by the iconoclasts, was attached again thanks to its intercession.

'Sleeplessness has traced a shadow ring'
This is the first of ten poems from *Milestones* included in the cycle 'Sleeplessness' in Tsvetaeva's collection *Psyche*. The others are 'I adore kissing', 'In this immense city of mine – night', 'After a night without sleep the whole body is weaker', 'Now I'm a heavenly guest', 'Tonight I'm alone in the night, a nun'. 'Oh how delicate

and faint', 'Dark as a pupil, and absorbing light', 'Who sleeps when night falls? Nobody can sleep!' and 'Look – another window'.

POEMS TO BLOK

1   In the old spelling used by Tsvetaeva, Blok's name had five letters, including the 'hard sign' at the end.

5   Beginning with Peter the Great, the Russian tsars were buried in St Petersburg. Until then, their final resting place had been the Cathedral of the Archangel in the Moscow Kremlin.

POEMS TO AKHMATOVA

2   Tsar's Village or Tsarskoye Selo, outside St Petersburg, has strong literary associations with Pushkin and Annensky as well as with Akhmatova. The Catherine and Alexander palaces are located there. Known as Children's Village in Soviet times, today it forms part of the town of Pushkin.

4   Tsvetaeva's words about 'an appalling legacy' came to seem prophetic. Lev Gumilyev (1912-1992), Akhmatova's son by the poet Nikolay Gumilyev, who was executed by a firing squad in 1921 on trumped-up charges of a monarchist conspiracy, became a historian and ethnographer. He spent most of the years between 1938 and 1956 in labour camps.

8   The celebrated monastery of the Trinity, founded by St Sergey of Radonezh, is situated about 45 miles northwest of Moscow. Tsvetaeva published an essay about the women of the sect of the Khlysts or Flagellants in 1934.

9   'Golden-lipped' is the meaning of the name normally given to St John Chrysostom (c.349-407) on account of his famed eloquence.

'After a night without sleep the whole body is weaker'
Tsvetaeva and Efron did not in fact stop in Florence on their honeymoon travels in 1912.

'A female adventurer, a man'
Corinna and Oswald are characters from Madame de Staël's novel *Corinne*, first published in 1807.